# *Easy* Keyboard Harmony

## Book One

### by Wesley Schaum

## Foreword

This series provides practical keyboard training leading into improvising and accompaniment from standard chord symbols... those commonly found in pop, folk, country and sacred music... the same as used for guitar, organ, chord organ and piano accordion.

A background of at least Level Two pianistic ability is necessary before starting this book. The Schaum *"Scale Speller"* is recommended as a prerequisite or supplement.

In this first book, root position major and minor triads plus 7th chords are explored in seven common tonalities. A variety of accompaniment styles in both 4/4 and 3/4 meter are written and played, using well-known folk songs, hymns and other melodies as illustrations.

Ear training is to be encouraged. A very desirable side-effect of study in this book is to implant the *sound* of various major, minor and 7th chords into memory. Harmonic analysis is purposely avoided. It is intended that practical keyboard experience be allowed to develop prior to analytical work.

Extra books and sheet music with chord symbols should be used as supplements after finishing Lesson 14. Choices should be limited to the vocabulary of chords shown on the front inside cover. Specific suggestions are found in that location.

## Contents

EXCLUSIVELY DISTRIBUTED BY

HAL•LEONARD®
CORPORATION
7777 W. BLUEMOUND RD. P.O. BOX 13819 MILWAUKEE, WI 53213

© Copyright 1981 & 1982 by Schaum Publications, Inc., Mequon, Wisconsin
International Copyright Secured • All Rights Reserved • Printed in U.S.A.

ISBN-13: 978-1-936098-55-2

## LESSON 1: C and G Major Triads

A *triad* is a three note chord built by using the 1st, 3rd and 5th degrees of any major scale. The chord name comes from the bottom note, called the *root*. The line below shows how the C major triad is formed:

      1st    measure:  first five notes of the C major scale
      2nd   measure:  1st, 3rd and 5th degrees of the C major scale
      3rd    measure:  C major triad (block chord)
4th & 5th  measures:  triad variations (broken chords)

**Directions:** Practice the following line at least five times per day until it can be played easily and accurately. For extra practice, play the same line one octave lower.

**Directions:** The line below shows how the G major triad is formed. Practice this line at least five times per day until it can be played easily and accurately. For extra practice play the same line one octave higher.

**Attention:** The capital letter "C" is the *chord symbol* (musical abbreviation) of the C major triad. Likewise, "G" is the chord symbol for the G major triad. These chord symbols appear above the treble clef melody notes in the following piece of music.

**Directions:** Learn to play "Lightly Row" (below) using the block chord accompaniment shown.

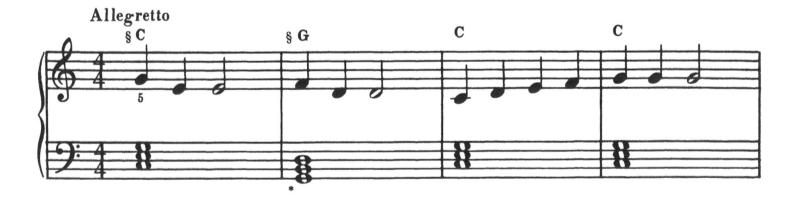

**\*Spinet Organ Note:** If the lower keyboard does not include low G, play this one octave higher.

**§Organ Pedal Instructions:** Play the root (bottom note) of each triad and sustain it for a full measure.

# LESSON 1 - continued

There are many different ways of using a triad for an accompaniment. This page illustrates two rhythmic variations of the basic block chords presented on page 2.

**Directions:** Study the accompaniment variation in the first line of "Lightly Row". Write the same style accompaniment in the 2nd line.

## LIGHTLY ROW

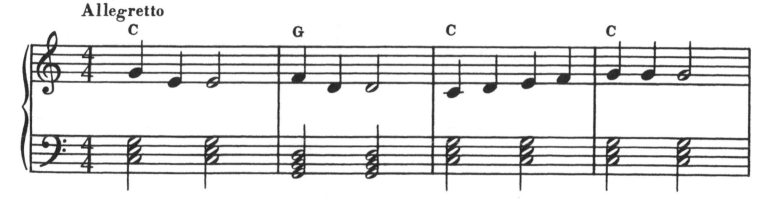

**Directions:** Study the accompaniment variation in the 3rd line of "Lightly Row" (below). Write the same style accompaniment in the 4th line. Then learn to play the entire piece.

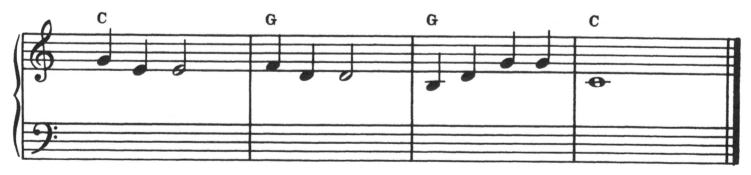

**Attention:** It is important that you *memorize* the accompaniment variations on this page and also all others encountered as you progress in this book. The purpose is to build a "vocabulary" of variations that you can use later when improvising your own accompaniments for pieces outside of this book.

4

## LESSON 2: F Major Triad

**Directions:** The line below shows how the F major triad is formed. Practice this line at least five times per day until it can be played easily and accurately. For extra practice, play the same line one octave higher.

**Directions:** Study the accompaniment written in the first line of "SKIP TO MY LOU" (below). Write the same style accompaniment in the 2nd line. Then learn to play both lines. (For variety, the F major triad may be played one octave higher.)

**Directions:** Study the accompaniment written in the first line of "THIS OLD MAN" (below). Write the same style accompaniment in the 2nd line. Then learn to play both lines.

*Spinet Organ Note: If the lower keyboard does not include low F or G, play the F and G accompaniments one octave higher.

# LESSON 3: 4/4 Accompaniment Variations

**Directions:** Study the new accompaniment written in the first line of "Jingle Bells". Write the same style accompaniment in the 2nd line.

**JINGLE BELLS**

**Directions:** Study the new accompaniment written in the next line of "Jingle Bells". Write the same style accompaniment in the last line. Then learn to play the entire piece.

**Attention:** The notes indicated by a chord symbol are *not* affected by any key signature. Therefore, key signatures have been omitted from all bass staffs beginning with this page. The G major chord (in 2nd line, above) is played with a B-natural, even though the key signature for the melody has a B-flat.

## LESSON 4: Review of Accompaniment Variations

**Directions:** Choose any one accompaniment style from those shown above. Write the accompaniment for the first two lines of **"BLUE TAIL FLY"** (below). Next, choose and write a *different* style for the last two lines. Then learn to play the entire piece.

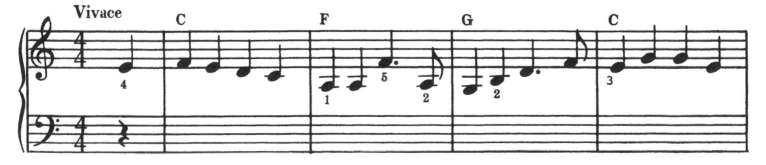

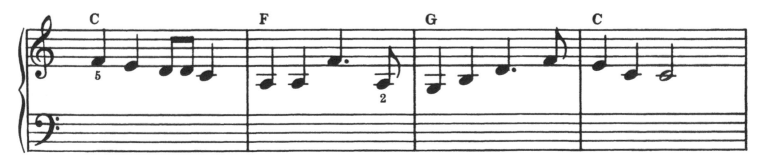

**Organ Note:** A melody with very low notes, such as "Blue Tail Fly" usually sounds better when played one octave higher. If it is played as written do not use any 16′ stops for the upper keyboard.

# LESSON 4 - continued

**Directions:** The line below shows different octave positions for the C, F and G major chords. Before writing in the accompaniment on this page, experiment by playing each chord in *both* octave positions. Choose the position that moves most easily to and from adjoining chords . . . and which sounds best. Of course, avoid a position that would interfere with playing the treble clef melody notes.

**Directions:** Choose any one accompaniment style from those at the top of page 6. Write that accompaniment for the 1st and 3rd lines of "Golden Slippers". Next, choose and write a different style for the 2nd and 4th lines. Then learn to play the entire piece.

## GOLDEN SLIPPERS

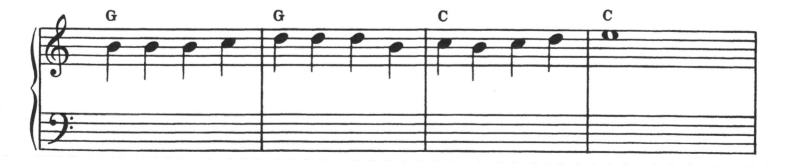

## LESSON 5:  D Major Triad

**Directions:** The line below shows how the D major triad is formed. Practice this line at least five times per day until it can be played easily and accurately. For extra practice, play the same line one octave lower.

**Directions:** Study the accompaniment written in the first two measures of "CAMPTOWN RACES" (below). Write the same style accompaniment through the end of the 2nd line of music.

**Directions:** Study the new accompaniment written in the first two measures of the line below. Write the same style accompaniment for the remainder of the piece. Then learn to play the entire piece.

# LESSON 6: Chord Changes on 3rd Count

Many pieces of music have two or more different chords in the same measure. With the block chord accompaniment used in the first two lines of this piece, it means jumping from one chord to another more frequently.

**Directions:** Study the accompaniment written in the first two measures of "Shoo Fly". Look for the chord changes on the 3rd count of some measures. Write the same style accompaniment through the end of the 2nd line.

**SHOO FLY**

**Directions:** Study the accompaniment written in the next two measures of "Shoo Fly". Write the same style accompaniment for the remainder of the piece. Then learn to play the entire piece.

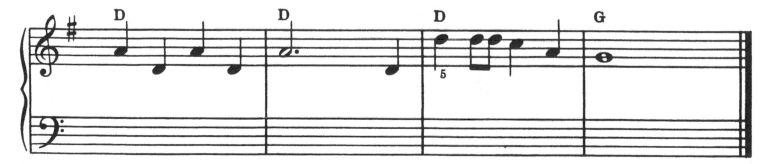

**Organ Pedal Instructions:** When there is a change of chord on the 3rd count, the pedal must change to root of the new chord.

10

# LESSON 7: Chord Changes with Broken Chord Accompaniment

The broken chord accompaniment to be used on this page is shown above. However, in measures where there is a chord change, you will be able to play *only the first two counts* of each broken chord pattern, as illustrated in the line below:

**Directions:** Write the complete accompaniment for **"NEARER, MY GOD, TO THEE"**, using the same style shown above. Watch for measures with chord changes. Then learn to play the entire hymn.

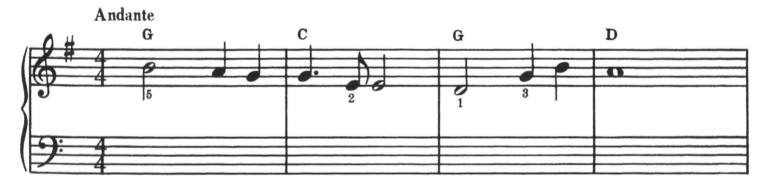

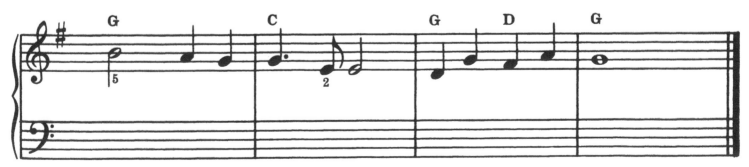

# LESSON 7 - continued

The broken chord accompaniment to be used on this page is shown above. However, in measures where there is a chord change, you will be able to play *only the first two counts* of each broken chord pattern, as illustrated below:

**Directions:** Write the complete accompaniment for **"SWING LOW SWEET CHARIOT"**, using the style shown above. Watch for measures with chord changes. Then learn to play the entire piece.

Moderato

12

## LESSON 8:  B-flat Major Triad

**Directions:** The line below shows how the B-flat major triad is formed. Practice this line at least five times per day until it can be played easily and accurately. For extra practice, play the same line one octave higher.

**Directions:** Study the accompaniment written in the first two measures of "HUSH LITTLE BABY" (below). Write the same style accompaniment for the remainder of the piece. Then learn to play both lines of music.

**Directions:** Study the accompaniment in the first two measures of "GO TELL AUNT RHODY" (below). Write the same style accompaniment for the remainder of the piece. Then learn to play both lines of music.

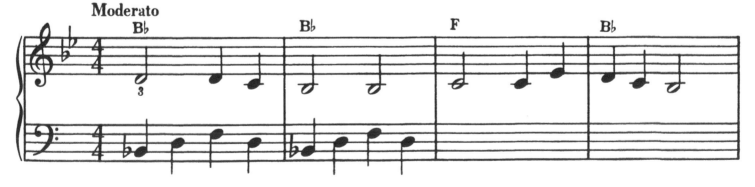

# LESSON 9: Accompaniment in 3/4 Meter

Any chord can also be played in 3/4 meter. This lesson presents two different accompaniment styles for 3/4 time.

**Directions:** Study the new accompaniment written in the first three measures of "Lavender's Blue". Write the same style accompaniment through the end of the 2nd line.

## LAVENDER'S BLUE

**Directions:** Study the new accompaniment written in the next three measures of "Lavender's Blue". Write the same style accompaniment for the remainder of the piece. Then learn to play the entire piece.

**Reminder:** The notes indicated by a chord symbol are *not* affected by any key signature. Therefore, key signatures have been omitted from all bass staffs. The G major chord (in the 2nd line, above) is played with a B-natural, even though the key signature for the melody has a B-flat. Also, be sure to write an *accidental* B-flat for every B-flat chord.

# LESSON 10:  A Major Triad

**Directions:** The line below shows how the A major triad is formed. Practice this line at least five times per day until it can be played easily and accurately. For extra practice, play the same line one octave higher.

**Directions:** Study the new accompaniment written in the first two measures of "SANTA LUCIA" (below). Write the same style accompaniment through the end of the 2nd line. Be sure to include the necessary sharps (chords are *not affected* by the key signature).

**Directions:** Study the new accompaniment written in the next two measures of "Santa Lucia". Write the same style accompaniment for the remainder of the piece. Then learn to play the entire piece.

## LESSON 11: Review of 3/4 Accompaniment Variations

**Directions:** Choose any one accompaniment style from those shown above. Write that accompaniment for the 1st, 2nd and 4th lines of **"AMAZING GRACE"** (below). Next, choose and write a different style for the 3rd line. Then learn to play the entire hymn.

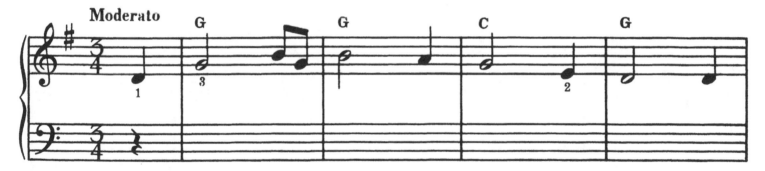

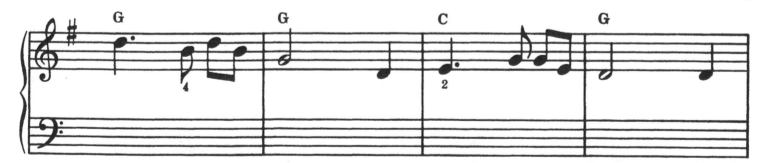

*****Organ Accompaniment Note:** For added variety these chord patterns may be played using *pedal alone* on the *first count.* The left hand would play notes of the 2nd and 3rd counts on the lower manual.

## LESSON 12: E-flat Major Triad

**Directions:** The line below shows how the E-flat major triad is formed. Practice this line at least five times per day until it can be played easily and accurately. For extra practice, play the same line one octave lower.

**Directions:** Write the accompaniment for the 1st and 3rd lines of "The More We Get Together". Use the same style as in the first measure of the 1st line. Next, write the accompaniment for the 2nd and 4th lines, using the same style as in the first measure of the 2nd line. Then learn to play the entire piece.

**Reminder:** Be sure to include accidentals for all B-flats and E-flats in the accompaniment.

### THE MORE WE GET TOGETHER

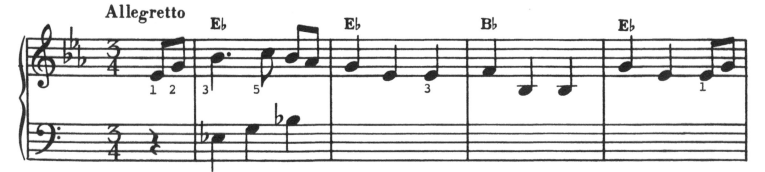

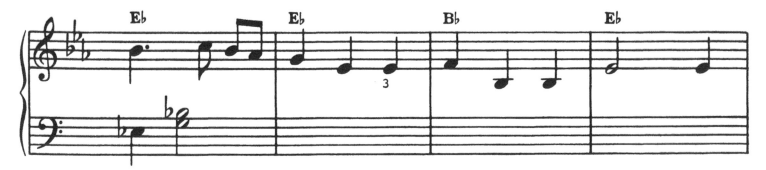

# LESSON 13:  Review of 4/4 Accompaniment Variations

**Directions:** Experiment by playing several different accompaniment styles from those shown above, with the 1st and 3rd lines of "America the Beautiful". Write the one you like best in both lines. Do the same for the 2nd line but choose a different style. Also do the same for the 4th line but choose another style. Then learn to play the entire piece.

This pattern of alternating three different accompaniment styles every four measures can be used for many pieces of music and also can be adapted to 3/4 meter.

## AMERICA THE BEAUTIFUL

# LESSON 14: Minor Triads

Any major triad can be changed into a *minor* triad by lowering the middle note one chromatic half-step, as illustrated below. The chord symbol for a minor triad is a small letter "m" placed beside the usual chord letter name.

**Directions:** Practice the line above at least five times per day until it can be played easily and accurately. Next, write the accompaniment for the first two lines of "GREENSLEEVES" (below). Use the same block chord style as in the first measure.

**Directions:** Write the accompaniment for the next two lines of "Greensleeves". Use the same style as in the first measure, below. Then learn to play the entire piece.

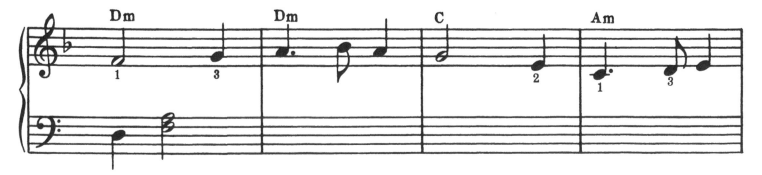

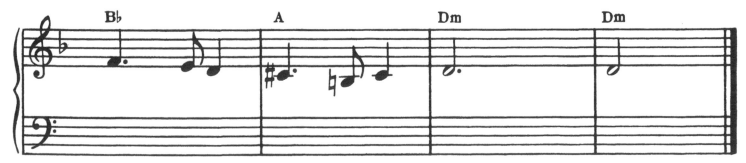

# LESSON 14 - continued

**Directions:** Broken chord accompaniments are shown above for five minor chords. Practice the line above at least five times per day until it can be done easily and accurately.

Write the accompaniment for the first two lines of "Black Is the Color of My True Love's Hair". Use the block chord style that appears in the first measure.

### BLACK IS THE COLOR OF MY TRUE LOVE'S HAIR

**Directions:** Write the accompaniment for the next two lines of "Black Is the Color . . . ". Use the broken chord style as shown in the first two measures, below. Then learn to play the entire piece.

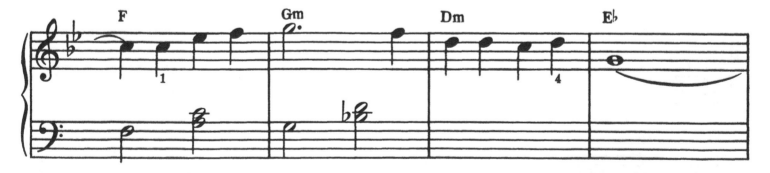

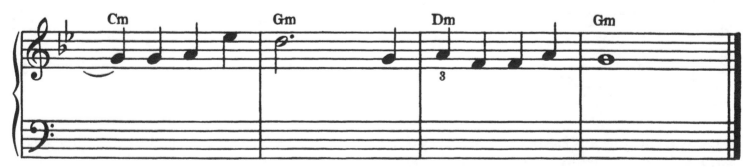

## LESSON 14:  Minor Triads - continued

**Directions:** Minor chords are shown above in a new accompaniment variation. Practice the line above at least five times per day until it can be done easily and accurately.

Write the accompaniment for the first two lines of **"MEADOWLANDS MARCH"** (below). Use the style shown in the first measure.

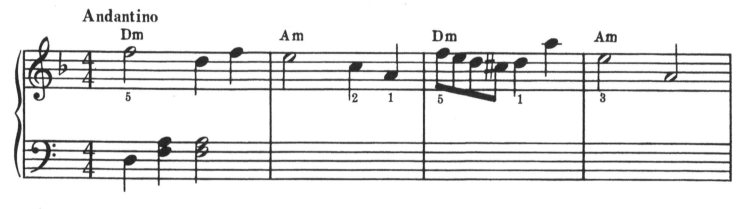

**Directions:** Write the accompaniment for the next two lines of "Meadowlands March". Use the style shown in the first measure, below. Then learn to play the entire piece.

**Reminder:** Any chord can be played one octave higher or lower than shown at the top of this page. Choose the octave position that fits most smoothly with adjoining chords.

# LESSON 14 - continued

**Directions:** Practice the line below at least five times per day until it can be played easily and accurately.

Before writing the accompaniments on this page, experiment by playing the chords at different octave positions. Find which positions fit best with adjoining chords and which sound best with the melody.

**Directions:** Write the accompaniment for all of **"JOHN HENRY"** (below). Use the same style that appears in the first measure. Then learn to play the entire piece.

It is assumed that the C chord in the next line (below) begins on the 3rd count (although the C chord symbol is not written directly above any note).

**Reminder:** Be sure to write all accidental signs necessary for bass clef chords.

Attention: In most albums and sheet music with chord symbols, it is common to eliminate chord symbols that are the same for more than one measure. Therefore, in measures that have no printed chord symbol you continue to play the previous chord until a new chord symbol appears. On this page and for the remainder of this book, the repeated chord symbols are printed. These chord symbols are usually omitted in most music.

# LESSON 15: Additional 3/4 Accompaniment Variations

**Directions:** Experiment by playing the first two lines of "Sweet Betsy from Pike" with several of the new accompaniment styles shown above. Write the style that seems to fit best with the melody.

### SWEET BETSY FROM PIKE

**Directions:** Experiment by playing the next two lines of "Sweet Betsy" using other accompaniment styles shown at the top of this page. Write a style that is *different* from that used in the first two lines. Then learn to play the entire piece.

# LESSON 16:  Additional 4/4 Accompaniment Variations

**Directions:** Experiment by playing the first two lines of "Shenandoah" with several of the new accompaniment styles shown above. Write the style that seems to fit best with the melody. Also experiment for the last two lines, but choose and write a different style accompaniment. Then learn to play the entire piece.

### SHENANDOAH

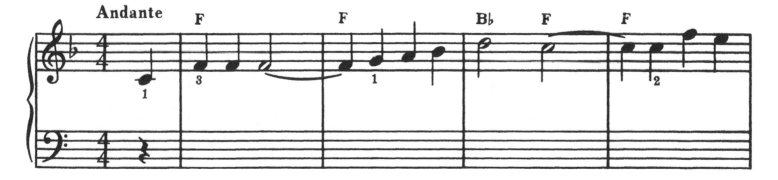

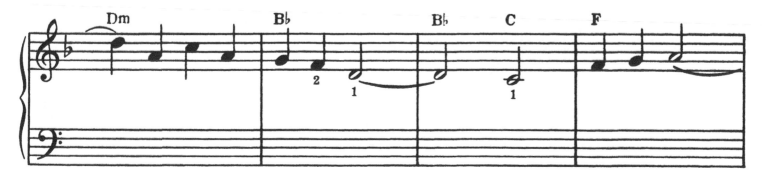

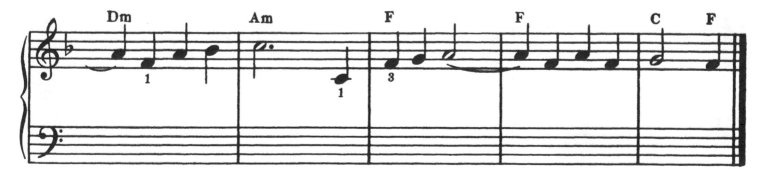

24

# LESSON 17: 7th Chords in 4/4 Meter

Any major chord can be changed into a 7th chord by adding one note 3 half-steps above the top note of the chord, as illustrated below. The chord symbol for a 7th chord is the number 7, placed beside the usual chord letter name.

**Directions:** Practice the line below at least five times per day until it can be played easily and accurately.

**Directions:** Write the accompaniment for the last three lines of **"BY THE MOON'S PALE LIGHT"** (below). Use the same style shown in the first line. Then learn to play the entire piece.

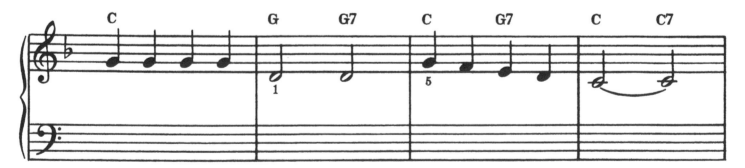

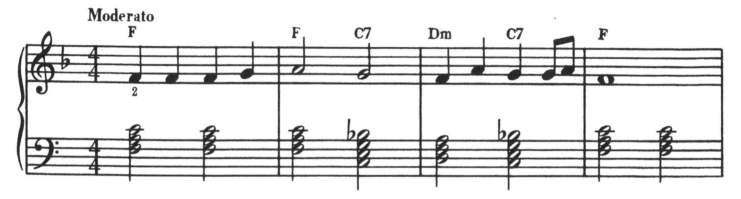

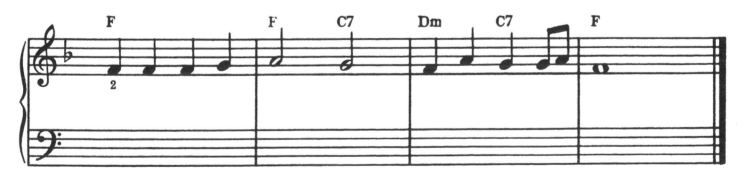

*Spinet Organ Note: If the lower keyboard does not include a low F or G, omit the root (bottom note) and play just the upper three notes of the F7 and G7 chords on the lower keyboard. Play the root of each chord in the pedal. This same idea could be used with other 7th chords for extra variety.

# LESSON 17 - continued

The line below shows how to play 7th chords as a broken chord accompaniment. This style is to be used in playing the piece on this page.

**Directions:** Practice the line below at least five times per day until it can be played easily and accurately.

**Directions:** Write the accompaniment for all of "Abide With Me". Use the same style as is found in the first two measures. Then learn to play the entire hymn.

## ABIDE WITH ME

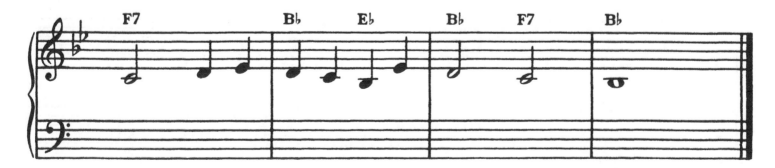

## LESSON 18:  7th Chords in 3/4 Meter

The line below shows 7ths as a broken chord accompaniment in 3/4 time.

**Directions:** Practice the line below at least five times per day until it can be played easily and accurately.

**Directions:** Write the accompaniment for all of "Heart of My Heart". Use the same style as in the first measure and in the line above. Then learn to play the entire piece.

### HEART OF MY HEART

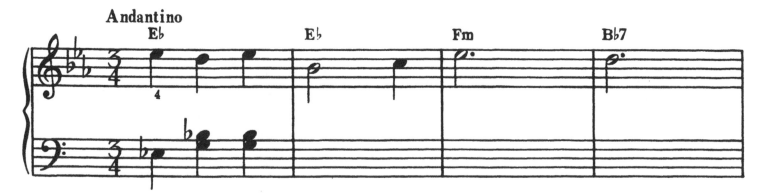

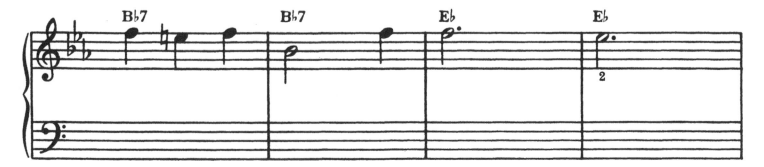

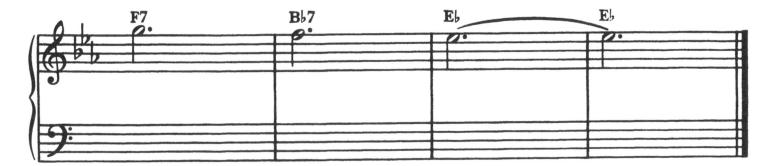

# LESSON 18 - continued

The line below compares block 7th chords to a new style of broken chord accompaniment. Notice that *one note is omitted* from the broken chord. The omitted note is the 2nd note from the *top* of the block 7th chord.

**Directions:** Practice the line below at least five times per day until it can be played easily and accurately.

**Directions:** Write the accompaniment for all of **"IN THE GOOD OLD SUMMERTIME"** (below). Use the broken chord style shown in the first measure and in the line above. Then learn to play the entire piece.

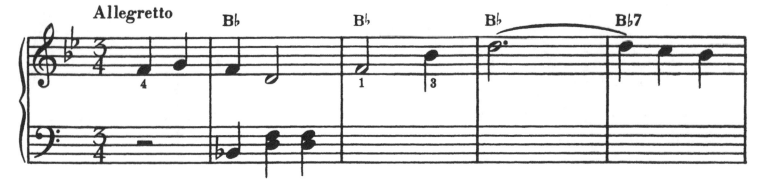

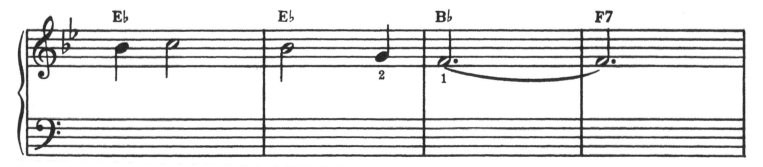

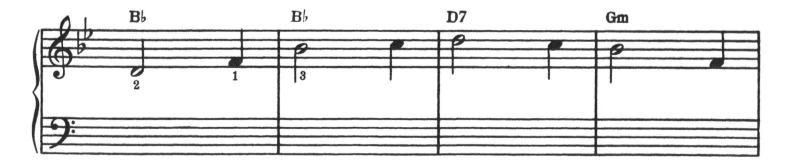

## LESSON 19: Broken 7th Chord Accompaniments

The line below shows how to omit one note of each 7th chord to form a broken chord accompaniment. The last measure shows how to make a chord change within the same measure.

**Directions:** Practice the line below at least five times per day until it can be played easily and accurately.

**Directions:** Write the accompaniment for all of **"AULD LANG SYNE"** (below). Use the style shown in the first measure. Then learn to play the entire piece.

# LESSON 19 - continued

The line below shows various 7ths as block chords but with one note omitted. Half note broken chord accompaniment variations are also illustrated.

**Directions:** Practice the line below at least five times per day until it can be done easily and accurately.

**Directions:** Write the accompaniment for **"IN THE EVENING BY THE MOONLIGHT"** (below). Use half note *broken chord* accompaniment for all measures with just one chord. Use half note *block* accompaniment where there are two chords in one measure. Then learn to play the entire piece.

# LESSON 19: Broken 7th Chord Accompaniments - continued

The line below shows 7ths as broken chord accompaniments in 3/4 time.

**Directions:** Practice the line below at least five times per day until it can be played easily and accurately.

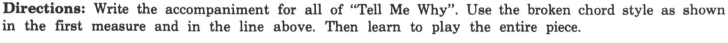

**Directions:** Write the accompaniment for all of "Tell Me Why". Use the broken chord style as shown in the first measure and in the line above. Then learn to play the entire piece.

## TELL ME WHY

# LESSON 20:  Review of 3/4 Accompaniment Patterns

The line below shows different styles of accompaniment for 3/4 time that have been presented in this book. Although written for the C major chord, these accompaniment patterns can be adapted to any chord.

**Directions:** Practice the line below at least five times per day until it can be played easily and accurately. Also try doing the same line but using other chords.

**Directions:** Experiment by playing at least four different accompaniment styles (from above) with the first two lines of "Cielito Lindo". Write the one accompaniment that seems to fit best with the melody.

## CIELITO LINDO

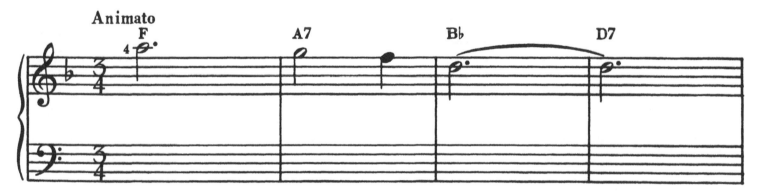

**Directions:** Experiment by playing additional accompaniment styles with the last two lines of "Cielito Lindo" (below). Write one that seems to fit well with the melody, but is not the same as chosen for the first two lines. Then learn to play the entire piece.

# LESSON 21: Review of 4/4 Accompaniment Patterns

The line below shows different styles of accompaniment for 4/4 time that have been presented in this book. Although written for the C major chord, these accompaniment patterns can be adapted to any chord.

**Directions:** Practice the line below at least five times per day until it can be played easily and accurately. Also try doing the same line but using other chords.

**Directions:** Experiment by playing at least four different accompaniment styles (from above) with the *first eight measures* of **"MY TASK"** (below). Write the one accompaniment that seems to fit best with the melody.

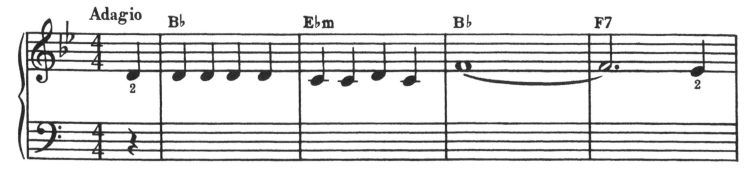

**Directions:** Experiment by playing additional accompaniment styles with the remainder of "My Task". Write one that seems to fit well with the melody, but is not the same as chosen for the first *eight measures*. Then learn to play the entire piece.

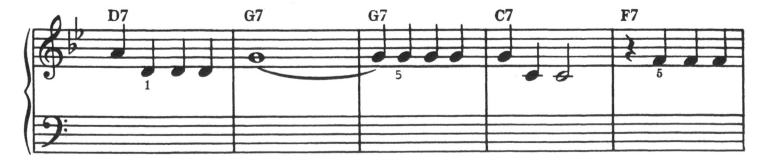

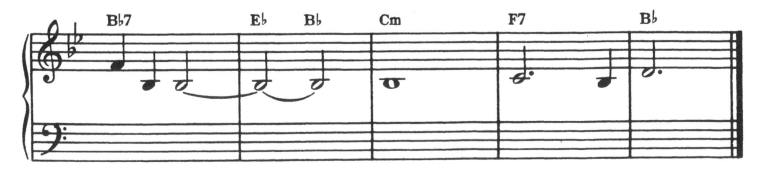